Poems For Leisure

NEERAJ CHAHAL

First published in 2020 by
BecomeShakespeare.com

One Point Six Technologies Pvt Ltd,
123, Building J2, Shram Seva Premises,
Wadala Truck Terminus,
Wadala (E), Mumbai - 400037
T:+91 8080226699

ISBN: 978-93-90463-65-7

My first ever book on poetry is dedicated to Annie Johnson from Indiana, USA. She inspired me to take my first step into the field of writing my inner thoughts. She is a person of a broad thinking and caring nature.

The Misty

3 Nov 2019

All around my eyes of the soul,

I, am opaque fog, observe.

Worse than darkness at night

That disables me, nerve to nerve.

May be, by too much pollution,

Cowset by irrelevant anger.

Was the blinding thing brought,

Forming to my spirit, as danger.

Range of thinking enclosed

Nothing good I currently do.

No positive thoughts allowed,

The fog forbids me see-theory.

My mind made up, I say this,

"Come Heavenly Rains, to wash out.

For the sake of my pious being,

Never shall I my pride flout.

To preserve our holy spirit,

It to live a meaningful time.

Dispelling away fogs of sorts,

Giving the soul, a human shine!

Ravaged

Nov, 19
The snakes of sorrow,
Hissing at my soul.
The fire of love to you,
Has reduced to ash ball.
No sooner did I learn,
Of your cheating on me.
Than, came a tearful surge,
Sinking joys into a valley.
Come, o ever growing pain,
In my soul, to ignite.
Take me back to wher3e,
With odds, love did fight.
Let in her memory, my die.
And build towers of love high.

Wisdom

4 Nov, 19
Sad and lonely,
In my true heart.
Walked I along,
A grassland vast.
A three-legged rat,
In a hole I saw.
Coming to take shine,
Of the sun, rising raw.
Can I not do,
What I now ought?
Learnt from that,
Glad I came with a thought.
A small creature,
At times does this.
Imparting you will,
To swim like a fish.
When the waters
Are pretty troubled.
You need a push,
To pass power-doubled.

Close To Me

Living on some where far,
In a world of your own.
Of course, my dear, you are,
Leaving my caring lips alone.
As a pleasant breeze blew,
Carrying with it sweet smell.
My hopes more strongly grew,
That me you missed well.
The nights here are long,
As I have no rest or sleep.
Echoes in my ears, the song,
Sung by you with voice deep.

With a faithful heart, I adore,
The beauty, once was at my door!

Balancedd

5-10-19

Never shall I find,

Such a lover as you.

With whom, my mind

Well with the heart grew.

Whenever it was doubt,

Shadowing my grimy head.

You helped me let out

Negating ideas, feelings bad.

The way you dispelled.

Dispair from this heart.

Is but a disguised boon,

Too good to me to part.

Love being, not merely a physical hot

Has power to change worst to best.

Pole Star

6-11-19

Everyday in the sky,

A star in North.

Gives me a lesson,

Too useful to be lost.

Being fixed at will,

To it, a value adds.

And makes it special,

For men of wise heads.

A man of purpose,

Human and good-will.

Constant at its place,

Can break a rocky hill.

Whether in solitude or in crowd.

Be adamant for the general good.

The Inner me

7 Nov, 19

Each morning brings me,

A hope for things I want.

The things, good to us all,

From my goodness do start/

In the course of passing,

My day many errors has.

May be distracted by flows,

This mind of mine, goes rash.

Then comes another night,

Taking with it, a new lesson.

And to me an insight gives.

In the faults, reared in passion.

Lost in the evaluation of daily doings,

Asleep I fall, to start a new morning.

Let us Be

8 Nov, 19

It was only yesterday,
Inseparably mingled, we were.
No fear of worldly loss,
Or joy to gain was there.
Odds crossed our union,
An ever-growing pain to give.
Even easier it is to die,
Than, to without love, live.
Of all the joys shared,
Many will forever last.
Life that was going slow,
Shall as Time fly fast.
Till the world to an end gets,
The heart will miss love in death.

Mood-swings

9 Nov, 2019

Pensive and angry inside,

I, was, once over something.

On a wall in my yard,

A monkey, I saw, over-hanging.

My eyes drawn to that,

Another one came to the first.

Mischief in its sharp eye,

Caused the player to hit earth.

Thud, was the sound heard,

Making my angry eyes smile.

Tension remained with me long,

Gone into air in the mean----

A watch-over to simple pranks,

To us may bring cheer and thanks.

Honey-moon

19 Nov, 19

Our first night together.

No less than Euphoria.

Came up like a boon,

Set to create insomnia.

Bodies to each other clung,

A union, our souls achieved.

For better ecstasy proved,

Than what I earlier believed.

Amid the noises of crowd,

Lovers of joy in bed moaned.

Losing our human selfs,

Were we in bliss drowned.

That warmth of purest passion,

Sleepless nights got to be fashion.

11 Nov, 19

Easy-going

Free from the daily acts,
A slow walk through country side.
Every evening do I take,
With mother Nature as a guide.
The sun going down in the west,
I the tired formers greet.
Trying to put balm on faces,
Dusted from work, and noon heat.
The cooing of cuckoo being faint,
Owing to crying all the day.
Makes me smile, as I gaze,
At the stars gathering in play.
The sound of fish in the pond,
Creates to placidity a might bond.

Teaching Myself

11 Nov, 19

This very question on my mind,

Sometimes, my heart, erodes.

What is purest human joy?

And what in life do the gods!

The answer to this teaser,

At right time, comes itself.

When I eat and sleep well,

And to odds don't whelp.

Peace of soul thurely occur4s,

After I have kept quiet.

Free from bondage of anger,

Act I wisely, thinking right.

Potience and restraint of pretty kind.

Are the source of a perfect mind.

Rain on Me

11 Nov, 19

Alas! The tree of my heart,
Suffered from a lack of water.
Long Since showed by love,
And by you slept under.
Dusted by winds of doubts
And parched by heat of anger.
Now appeasing like a ghost,
This dying thing is in danger.
Come rains of your passion,
All washed up it will be.
New flowers of true smiles,
And fruits of Eternal glee!
Water my roots in the soul,
Pruning the branches over all.

Wow! Tonight!

11Nov,19

The pretty moon, this night,
Prettier than ever will be:
Not because she ought to,
But owing to Gangetic glory:
Indians of faith in Mothers,
As a font to lovely life.
Will with holy waters wash,
And moonlight in youth ripe!
Millions of souls, even sinful,
Under the moon dip tonight.
To be blessed with purity,
Offer themselves to elixir white.
Beauty and perfection be to them,
That perpetualise Nature's fame.

Evolution

12 Nov, 19

Let me, to odge of doom,

Love you in my own way.

For rest or food no room,

Let lupid his game play.

You in my strong arms,

A safe haven shall find.

My cold heart in your warmth,

Will leave even angels behind.

Drinking in essence of souls,

We, in love, will be forever.

Be it storms or fire balls,

Still shall our saga be here.

For from formal deeds of sorts,

Let us travel to Paradise Lost.

To Ideal Land

13 Nov, 19

'Browning or keats or Gray,
Never do I think, could be.
Meant for you, my passion gay.
Is to me, the sacred poetry.
Mozart and Beethover, I do like,
For their devotion to breath.
When my heart, your eyes strike,
The holiest tune does generate.
Vinci and Raphael, of course,
To the world, are Art-giants.
Your velvet body, morning rose,
Makes up for faults, ancient.
Heat in cold and shade in desert,
Garden of dreams, shall Love birth.

Never Dying fire

13 Nov, 19

Tripping along the street,

Of loneliness and memory.

Sing each heart beat,

An ever- lasting symphony.

The evening with candles,

That on our table burnt.

The mornings of red ripples,

Shining with sunrays slant.

There were even timer,

When one were towo bodies.

A treasure for rhymes,

More sacred than hollies.

Wish I do for times to return,

In this fire, my cold sighs burn.

Children's Day

14 Nov, 19

Pretty flowers in God's garden,
Children are pure in souls.
Source of joy to their guardian,
Coloful like billards balls.
Now over this, making a row,
Then by consent, play together.
Simple joys give them a glow,
And sorrows touch them never.
Innocent of their faults too,
Children to novelty are eager.
Full of energy, they dream a new.
Wishing for games to run forever.
Indifferent to rich and poor,
They are blessed with moral air.

I Wish

15 Nov, 19

Hard it is to tell,

How badly I miss you!

Your eyes ring a bell.

In my soul turning blue.

A beautiful dream I had,

Last night with you there.

Tho' the morning few bad,

Not to have it my share.

Pretty like an anger.

Came you in my arms.

Kissing me with lips petal

Of your soft rosy woarmth.

A Virtuous Feel

16 Nov, 19

Love to me, no doubt,

Is but a special thing.

When of joys, run I out,

I gives a cheerful ring.

At times, I feel down,

Owing to pains, life gives.

Seeing lovers makes a clown,\

And brings so ungent relief.

Even in rags, or a rustic,

Every minute I do Smile.

An ascetic life for practice,

Love becomes a life style.

In times of financial want,

As is seen in human life.

Songs of love, do I chant,

And bliss becomes my type.

True, it is indeed, o men.

For me, you and us all.

Let love be a pleasant rain,

And upon us profitably fall.
Love, if felt in purest sense,
Would the beauty of soul, enhance!

An Ideal passion

Last night, was the best,
Of all nights so far.
Of joy, we made a fest,
Being observed of your body,
I unguided happily toured.
Gardens of velvet, rosy,
Surround a valley pleasant.
A journey through your eyes,
To the land of pretty dreams.
Came to an end, the sighs,
I used to have for guams.
Those perfect handsome curves,
Where I my head rested.
Are a shelter for my hurt,
And my tongule you nested.
Ecstasty to me till now,
Was but a popular word.
Making love to you wow!
Proved to be true expert.

Wild over All

On the bed of delicate grass,
Lay naked, two people love.
Lips locked in a magnetic mass
Her hands searching for joy, above.
Hot breaths giving ignition,
To the fuel of wild passion.
His hands gripping in obsession,
She was learning a new lesson.
Breast Nipples in joy taut,
She a crazy shriek screamed.
As he enter the alley soft.
And with blies her check gleamed.
Rocking on this merry go round,
A dreamland they both realized.
Real pleasure in each other found.
As the roses looked on surmised.
Damp with sweat of pure work,
A paradise today they had made.
To hell with sorrow and hurt,
Words of contentment they said.

Nov 19

Universal

People of the world,

Say if I am wrong.

Love being just a word,

Life is but a said song,

Really lucky you are,

Finding a caring love,

You being a bright star,

Inter vast sky above,

Definition of love varies,

For every human being,

To some it's a fine breeze,

And to many useless thing.

When your feel a joy in oter,

Love is happeningin true colors.

20 Nov Wed 19

All Except us

Every evening to me dear,

Brings many vision of you,
Looking ever fresh and fair,
To me you came as new,
The tree we sat under,
Arm in arm for hours.
Has lost its green cover,
And for us sheds tears,
The lake our sunset site
Has come to be just a pond,
Still the times of twilignt
Pull me over to cry alone.
The star of evening comes up yonder
That hinted at time to go asunday.

21 Nov 19 Thursday
My Precious gens

A source fo fatherly joy,
And pride for my eyes.
Never did I crave for a boy,

So dear is my girls price.
Cute and lovely like flowers,
All my house they illuminate.
Upon them my affection showers,
This very heart of bestest grade.
Clothed and washed by Mom,
Always do they attend school.
Ringing with laughter their home,
To them rest is not cool,
Hopscotch crom and jungle Bir,
Are their favorite with a drowin.

22 Nov 19 Friday
Breaking Childhood

Out in the burning sun,
Works there this poor boy.
Picking rags, his only fun,
Garbage dac the holy toy.
Homeleso and wandering child,

Does this all to boy bread,
Like a rabbit in the wild,
Get chased by wolves bad.
Ragged face and worn clothes,
Are his simple identity,
Dusty cold risky foot paths,
Being to him, only luxury.
A slap on the faccs of the rich,
His condition is but a cruel bitch,

22 Nov 19 Friday
You And You Only
The heart and its wishes,
Without you are nothing.
Just like my airy kisses,
Get lost in separating ringh.
Som many dreams decorated
In your lovein my eyes,
A paradise by passion illuminated,
And innumerable deepest signs.

A random knock at the door
Startles me from reverie.
Life now being nasty bore,
Round me I darkniss see.
Patience is what gives me peace
When agony bends me to knees.

Nov 24 Sunday

Thou Knoweth All
O father, Lord of all,
To you I urgently Pray.
Never make me too tall,
To play with
And kindly, God the father
On me bestow, sweetness
So never be I vulgar,
In my words in distress.
My soul you know best
Your command being my fatc.

Never let me be fondest
In calling myself most great.
Fet my heart be full of pride,
For India my father land's bride.

Simple As This

26 Nov, 19

In the very temple of my soul,

As my god, do you reside

Never have I faith in an idol,

Dark in me lit with a light.

As a hymn to praise you,

My signs melodiously serve.

No care if false or true,

As these eyes moistened blur.

Enlightened am I now in you,

You being my ultimate goal.

Devotion infinite as skies blue,

Ecastasy comes at beck and call.

Even sorrow here has no place,

Away it runs, on seeing your faced!

Long nights with no sleep,

And an aching lonely heart.

Accompany me as I weep,

Overdoing the lover's part.

Moments spent by us together,

In our union, though s----

Burn my soul like a splinter,
Taking toll on cotton bundle.
Still in every breath shallow
Her perfume my nose fills.
All pain does memory swallow,
As glass a stone kills.
Come tonight or let me die,
Hard it is five on a lie.

Merged

27 Nov, 19

Meaningless is my life,

If by you it's not shared.

As fruits don't get ripe,

If not to sun bared.

Death is just a word,

With you in my soul.

Such is the Eternal bird,

Never hunted by Time's toll.

The Storm Rider

27 Nov, 19

(Dedicated to massie Williams in Game of Throns.)

Here's a girl, Arya Stark,

A person of leonine vigor.

An indelible beautiful mark,

Be----- the family honor.

Curelty on her innocence,

Was by misfortune forced.

Taking away angelic cadence,

When Lannistess were endorsed.

Fierce as a hungry wolf,

And cleverer than a fox.

Never did she make dolls,

As for beds, having rocks.

Full of revenge upon the devils,

This baby ultimately the proud kills.

Pleasure

28 Nov, 19

Ice cold winds outside,

Made me shiver a lot.

A good reason to hide,

With you on a wooder cot.

Rubbing to your warmth,

Covered in a woolen sheet.

Taking you in my arms,

Brought me a cozy heat.

Passionate love we made,

All through the rainy night.

Bare our souls we laid,

To make life sacred light.

Splash of rain went along,

As we sang an eternal song.

Confluence

29 Nov, Fri

Into the lake of your eyes,

My love, let me drown.

Where swim, dreams rainbow,

Prettier than Peacock's crown.

Let me that nectar drink,

That your rosy lips fills.

May be, thirsty in day mouth,

After this act, gets thrills.

If your warmth of embrace,

I forever wish to sleep.

And all my painful days,

Absorb with your joy so deep.

Unique must be this sacred affair,

Like lungs filled with purest air.

An Poor Me

30 Nov, 19

Once again, in my dream,

She, before me, stood smiling.

With the same lovable gleam,

On her angelic cheek shining

Millions of things to talk about,

There were on my eager mind.

Words I forced out of mouth,

Still couldn't a sound find.

Pretty were the naughty eyes,

Looking invitingly into mine.

And drew her I closely nice,

To kiss those lips so fine.

Our curious hearts beat frantic.

The alarm broke my vision romantic.

Eternally Trued

1 Dec, 19

There might be differences
Of opinions with your loves.
May be also some distances,
But it keeps cooing like doves.
Meeting after an age of time,
Brings to you, the same joy.
As it was while in prime,
You liked her as a boy.
Pain of separation or controversy
Are in love a natural phase.
Breaching all sorts of heresy,
It comes clean, winning the race.
Even after a change of worlds,
Never does love gare for hurts.

Pretty Woman

3 Dec, 19

Her smile southing enough,

For the sad to lose sorrow.

Her complexion ---- though,

No desire fairness to borrow.

The chest like a pair of hills,

Softly does she do her walk.

The Curved of ottsmmy heart fills

With more than what they talk.

Prettiest eyes on her face,

Can a dark heart brighten.

Clothing for her womanly grace,

More of her beauty heighten.

Care for all, with compassion mixed.

It's a pretty woman of exact passion.

Insecurity

4 Dec, 19

Alas! Twas the worst night,
For the innocent, pretty girl.
Taking advantage of poor light,
Did the devils vices hurt.
The bike broken on the way,
She her sister did inform.
Subdued by hungry wolves grey,
Violated she was by a storm.
Raped before being burnt alive,
Easily was the girl finished.
Eaten by wicked wolves five,
Untimely death the angel kissed.
Agonised are mournful parents,
Whose soul her voice rents.

To Be With You

5 Dec, 19

The crescent moon overhead,

And twinkling evening stars,

Memories past making me sad,

As to you r ride harsh.

Even my sensible horse,

Wants me to smile soon.

Jumping all broad gorges,

Being to me a prized boon.

Years of pain I'vespent,

Waiting for today to come.

To your love, my soul bent

The heart pounding, like a drum.

Soon enough, will we, two meet,

Walking together on Love street.

My Heaven

6 Dec, 19

Well, there is a place,

In your beautiful body.

Where ends my crazy race,

And living becomes a glee.

Meaningless is my love,

When for from this place.

Just a dull flowerless grove,

Like an idol with no face.

While this place is blooming

With roses of soft warmth.

All my delicate joys grooming,

Sail I to Paradise unharmed.

Even ruins into palaces growing start

As you throne me in your heart.

Simple As That

7 Dec, 19

Even without a mascara,

Or a made up eye-brow.

And no diamond tiara,

You look fair as snow.

No more costly creams,

Does your face require.

Every like the moon beams,

Lips are red as fire.

True beauty keats said,

In beholder's eyes lies.

Better than a jeweled jade,

Proves the simplicity nice.

Love is what makes things pretty,

Irrelevent to true or fake laity.

It Had To be

8 Dec, 19

Over there in a prison call,

Doing his time is a man.

Why so, simply can I tell,

He did what a broke can.

The girl he ever adored,

Left him for one with fortune

His pleadings made her borsed

Who spoke haughtily, a goon.

Tried the broke his best,

To forgo the selfish bitch.

Having in mind, no timely res.

He killed her and the rich.

The dreams, like glass are broken,

With a lover of feelings as fun.

Sons of India

9-12-2019

Leaving behind their own,

Do they go to serve India.

Guarding against the terror don,

Far from the social media.

Vowed to protect Moturland,

Frost and heat they face.

Missing their country friend

Glorifying the patriotic heroes,

Brings with it no fears.

Still crave for ripe mangoes,

For waiting mothers, shed tears.

Sacrificing comfort for us all,

The soldiers keep India growing tall.

Hold On, Man

11-12-19

An invisible light within,

A true pathfinder in dark.

Never leaves me groping,

For the right, human mark.

Sometimes in an angry mind,

Find I a burning fire.

This inner light in kind,

Does away the gloomy desire.

Moments of sorrow meaningless,

And raw passion thrive on.

When my words are careless,

About the sound's silly tone.

Keep in touch with the sacred soul.

Let, it be my ultimate goal.

Imperishable

12-12-19

Forever will my heart,
Used to loving an angel,
Go on riding the cart,
To where bliss is ample.
A home based on trust,
By faithfulness walled.
Shall my soul construct,
With doors of joys small.
Very little of togetherness,
Have, though, we cherished
A good deal of happiness,
Yet, two souls nourished.
May this bond of passionate love,
Higher than the heavens grow!
An Infinitely vast space,
And distance of light-years.
Keep from me the face,
For which I shed tears,
The wishes and desires
To be with her forever.

Keep stroking soul fires
Making me search everywhere.
Then comes the inner peace,
Helping my eager heart.
As approach flying bees,
To the hive, set apart.
Even in two distant worlds.
Our love blooms in new buds.

Transcendent

Dec, 2019

Sailing through universal air,
Love is ever all pervading.
Emitting its light everywhere,
Sorrow with joys serenading.
Natural in true character,
Comes it smiling to us all.
Being but a vital factor,
Love shields from moral fall.
Strong enough to fight odds,
Like a knight in armous.
Leading life to peaceful roads,
Subdues it foes as a chairmen.
People of the world, listen to me,
Love is from material bonds, free.

Divine Boom
19 Dec Thu 2019
She is a beautiful dream,
That has now come true.
On my shining as a gleam,

Dropping down like dew.
With her in my eyes,
Life now is all bliss.
Pretty lively at sunrise,
Sunset does her lips kiss.
Peace and rest in the soul,
Are from love true born.
Her body, like a stroll,
On flowers with no thorn.
My being is with her replete
As we walk the same street

Dec 20 Friday 2019
Together with

In this jungle of wilderness,
She serves as a haunt of peace.
Bringing in all her tenderness,
And makes life like lush trees
Purpose of life now I have,

In loving her beautiful truth.
So much of pleasure to rev,
Bound like hair in a brush.
Even death with her here,
Will me no troubles cause
Elixer drunk from love dear,
Never allows joys to pause.
True meaning of love is plain,
As in a desert drizzling rain.

Dev 21 Saturday 2020 Indescribable
Words are the verbal form,
Of the feelings born within
Searching for an easy norm,
To get out as sweet saying.
Such an expression of truth,
Hidden under layero of soul.
In my peom spoken rough,
Of my my love as a whole,
They I though possibly best,

To say what I want to
Yet there are many lift,
Emonions that regularly grew
Next time I write a verse,
Swrely shall it be power hence,

23 Dec Mon 19
When his mind couldn't guess.
"Pairs of happy lovers on life
I am counting by throwing leaves.

A Dream Run

Lying uneasy in my bed,
A crazy dream I saw.
Here was this bold- eagle,
Flying with a rat in its paw.
As it swooped past me ,
The rat on the ground fell.
There stood a huge demon,
At the place let me tell.
Toward me the giant come,
With his jaws wide- open.
Covering the small gap there,
As I naturally made a run.
Down the bedding I simply went,
While Trying to outrun the gaint,
25 Dec Wed 2019

Hail The lord

Let the bells jingle,
To welcome the birth.
Of our true savior,
Of the souls on earth.
Make the raindeer pull,
Hard on the sleighs.
May on Humanity shine,
Angelic serene light rays
A cake made with love,
Let us all share now.
Dance with Janta claus
Carols being sung low,
The world ought to hate sins.
Is said in Christmas dins.

26 Dec 2019
Shelter Me
Too busy at doing things,
To wald free and wild.
So badly did I miss you.

Mother Nature as your child.
A slow walk along the river,
Hearing the waters speak soft.
Took away all my pains,
That business had brought.
Yellow flowers in mustard crop
Andbirds singing moving notes.
Gave my over wrought head,
Peace filled in eternal pots.
Gazing at the infinitely vast sky,
Made me smile as clouds flew by.

27 Dec Fri 19
That Tiny Teacher:
Today, I, in my Yard,
Saw a spectacle fine.
Under the margosa tree.
Ants walked in a line.
One of them limped adon.
Due to extra took in hand.

It dragged with dedication,
One of its kids, to stand.
While doing this hard on,
It carried the grains too.
And never lost the track,
To its hill, to be true.
A great deal of wisdom we find.
If to minions, we are simply kind.
Once upon a time somewhere.
A prince out went for hunting.
By the riverside in the jungle
An old lady he saw, counting.
"What do you count?" asked he
When his mind couldn't guess.
"Pairs of happy lovers on life
I am counting by throwing leaves.

Closely Far

11-01-2020
Each morning, these days,
With a hope, I arise.
May be there will be,
My face in her eyes.
All my busy hours,
She dances in my mind.
Despite that, work I do,
As jobs are hard to find.
Once home to the sun-set,
Comes she wearing twilight.
Making promises beautiful
To visit me, in the night.
Dreams of her, in many forms,
Keep me awake, as do storms.

Vivekananda

12-01-20

As a boy, a naughty one,
Pranks he made for fun.
A pupil with inquiring mind,
Unseen facts eager to find.
Preacher of practical truth,
Never following superstitious.
To quench his thirst strong,
With Ramakrishna, went along.
The joy of wisdom, duly came,
And he got the perfect name.
A believer in theory of action,
Said he work for perfection.
Adorer to India his ----
Proved he in honour to her.
He shut the mouths of all,
In Chicago, speaking hall.
Alas, the world he left young,
Giving us thoughts of song unsung.

Something Good

28 Dec, 19

"Working in a frosted pond,
Is a sight I chanced to see.
On my walk the country side,
When after my day, I was free.
Fishing in the dirty water,
There were some poor kids,
Bodies weak with malnutrition,
Shivered like aspen against winds
Money for the house. By selling,
The catch they would earn.
That would for the hungry mom
Bring bread in its turn.
Giving them some coins I had,
Sent I them to buy bread.

1-02-20

Everlasting

Acroso the blue sky
Of my loving heart.
Hover with a thunder,
Clouds of pain stark.
Ever since you checked,
The waters of care.
Parched have been so,
Boughs of feeling fare.
On the stony paths,
Of loneliness dark.
Walks my tender love,
To follow constant mark.
May my soul forever now,
Never before suffering bow!

Finding You

2-1-20

Though you live far away,

In a land that I don't know.

My heart, yet feels you8,

Like an arrow, does a bow.

Mesmerised under your spell,

To you I am coming soon.

Rough terrains to be walked,

And for a light, a pale moon.

Asking the valleys and the lake

For my angel's nice home.

Submerged in the sea of love,

I, as a wanderer, ever roam.

Fear of death or joy of living,

To me become an irrational thing.

Fresh And Alive

4-1-20

While reading pretty did I see.

Dried, rose petals you put,

With my name penned nicely.

That me of times reminded,

When you for me waited.

Unable to express the love,

In your heart, decorated.

Though clearly I know not,

When we shared fiction stuff.

Yet your writing on petals,

Made me sure, was love.

How I wish, you'd been brave,

We would have had a treasure to save.

Arboreal Diva

5-1-20

Vibrant and fluttering,

Full of joy to live.

On flowers and seeding

With a lot to give.

To your present form,

Have you reached hard.

Ever since been born,

Never lost your heart.

Travelling all around,

You ever spread beauty.

Teaching all you found,

Discharge you the duty.

The ugly are by you inspired,

The pretty always are admired.

Small is Great

6-1-20

Show up as a fool,

If you want to be wise.

Embrace sorrow as a tool,

To be joyous, as body dies.

Be a loving heart,

To them who hate you.

That is but good start,

To a life, purely new.

Strive to render help,

Even when in want, you are.

Uncaring for amassed wealth,

That is useless like a scar.

Learn from what you wrong,

Sing for ecstasy, the holy song!

Just Watch

8-1-20

Love has different names,

For all who ever do.

It is meaningful when,

A butterfly kisses anew.

Love is most visible,

As it rains in summer.

The earth, long thirsty,

Get wet with pure elixir.

To a candle burning bright,

A moth dances buzzing.

Uncared for getting killed,

Her angel shine loving.

Sacred are the feelings here,

Of passion to beauty rare.

Mercy Pays

9-1-20

Amid the roar of the mob,

Heard, I the suppressed cries.

Of a child, almost killed,

Under the feet of selfish guys.

Stooping down, took I him,

To my haven, in ---------

Outside this liquor store,

Had it been left to die.

With God's grace sure

And my love for him.

The boy grew up fast

To be great to swim.

The champion in the world swim.

Supports me in the phase of age.

Love Divine

10-1-20

Whenever your pretty eyes,

I see, in my heart's glass.

The whole of my interior,

Begins to lose killing dark.

Thousands of rainbow dreams,

In my eyes, take shape.

Despite this hateful distance,

Our bodies passionately embrace.

To the land of perfect joy,

Where there is love, blooming.

Travel, we hand in hand,

With ecstasy, souls grooming.

Paradise is just an imagination,

To me, it exists in our elation.

Be witched

14-1-20

As cute as a rabbit,

You are dear to look at.

Never allowing me a bit,

Ever smarter than a cat.

Beauty contained in roses,

Seems faded before the cheek.

Magic in eyes deep black,

Makes me act like a freak.

All my sorrowful sighs,

Are by your smile colled.

See, how a lover of beauty,

Is by fascination ruled.

Soft and smooth, silky hair,

Let me kiss you, fair forever.

Stay Safe

15-1-20

The human soul is truly pure,

Never let it be defiled.

By distraction in the life,

Or be by pleasures beguiled.

Means of sorts, body earns,

By means of human vice.

Affecting the clean surface.

That lord gave fairly nice.

The fight-back with odds,

Gives the soul, perfect form.

Trees with roots strong,

Face fearlessly the wind-storm.

Saving the soul from sky devils,

Must be the cure of all ills.

Two As One

15-1-20

My sacred love for you,

Is no less than adoration.

Where the temple of Faith,

Stands tall, based on elation.

To each other, both of us

In many ways complement.

Now I am your savious,

And you become my tenent.

Same intense passion there,

In two pure caring souls.

As in my inwared eye,

Your light visibly rolls.

As each day meets a night,

So do lovers share, feeling bright.

An Easy Choiced

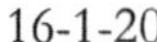

16-1-20

Pleased at my deeds good,

God offered me three boons.

Lots of wealth, or long life

Or a life with moral tunes.

Wealth for free being ill,

Would my life make waste.

Living longer with no peace,

Must be hell of worst taste.

Spending my numbered days,

No doubt, doing nice things.

Of course, should best prove,

An existence of human strings.

Thoughts I had considered well,

Short life of great acts so to tell.

One Life, One World

17-1-20

Let there be such a world,

As with no hateful thoughts.

Where love makes big trees,

To give shade in happy notes.

Where rivers flow clean,

Taking on productive waters,

And sky with pleasure blue,

Raining upon all sad quarters.

Here will be true heaven,

With caring angels inhibited.

No religion based permission,

Nobody in the temple prohibit

Envy, here, would get slain,

In my land, free from pain.

Time To Visit

18-1-20

Even spelling her sweet name,

To me brings a great thrill.

And my already crazy heart,

Goes on leaping like it will.

The mention of time we had,

Thou not much, is sufficient.

To keep me awake overnight.

Visualising reveries brilliant.

How can she not remember,

The night, when we one became.

Joy being showered upon us,

By stars in Cupid's name.

The Moon and the flowers here,

Do seek to meet, my dear!

Let me Not Wake Up

19-1-20

A pleasing sense of intoxication,

Felt I all the time today.

As yesterday night was a passion,

Making love in bed we lay.

Trying to find the real joy,

Bodies into a state sank.

Like a child for a lost toy,

Swims a river of overflowing bank.

That encounter of soft and hard,

Came as a struggle, undisguised

Similar to a wild leopard,

Being by a young cat surprised

Outspent, shivering in ecstasy,

To get up, we were too lazy.

Only You

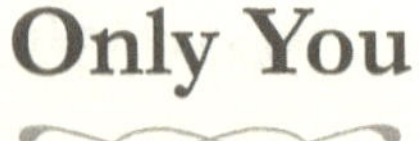

21-1-20

This crazy heart of mine,

Knows nothing but your love.

Thou there are beauties fine,

In my nest, you are the dove.

You, of course are other's

Of this, is my find sure.

From what my heart gathers,

My devotion to you is pure.

Yes, we'll never be on3e,

Like the scent in a rose.

See what my love's done,

Over all joys, you come close.

Just one good twist of lips,

Will be enough, for sinking ships.

Nothing Else Matters

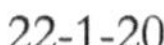

22-1-20

The joy in a peaceful soul,

Is the best joys among all.

An overtaking power it gives,

That in a moral abode lives.

All pains of ephemeral body,

Get forgone within a jiffy.

Troubles off you, start to flee,

On seeing the inward glee.

True meaning of life being this,

Knowing it is achieving bliss.

Try, so, to subdue the twister,

Raised in you by face character.

Once, this beauty you admire,

Sorrow will before its time expire.

Some Souls Speak

24-1-20

Whenever we casually meet,
There happens this something.
Restrictions off my mind fleet,
And the heart goes bling.
An urge to embrace you,
Takes a flight in my soul.
Suddenly, the vast sky blue,
Seems, to be as land to stroll.
From my desire of body,
You are free, it's true.
But in my romantic lobby,
I, all the time, savour you.
Never shall my love so pure,
Find a better healing cure.
Precious one:
The true purpose of life,
Is, I believe to save the soul.
Once my days are ripe,
Doing this should be foul.

To this world of varying hues,
Sent I was, clenched fist.
Amidst my joys and blues,
Happened, I, to ignore the gyst.
When from living, I retire,
Naught is what, goes beyond.
Wealth and fame I acquire,
Just to leave an empty bond.
So, from now on till I depart,
Soul-saving must to my chart.

Jai Ho, India

26-1-20

Owner of a brilliant past,

With moral values enriched.

Beautiful India in gold cast,

Was by robbers white hitched.

A long spell of exploitation,

Suffered at the hands of power.

She became the lewd passion,

To Europeans and Islam-herder.

Salute to the great children,

Mother bore, of heroic hearts.

Whose love for honor pristine,

Won back glory, lost in parts.

This century is of utmost progress,

In my motherland, envy to Empress.

Truly Yours

28-1-20

Lonely as the pole star,

You left me, other day.

For the so-called superstar,

Working as Chief of Ray.

But my innocent feeling,

Daily asks me a question.

Why for the faithless crying,

Who took, you for fun?

Here is my simple reply,

To the eroding querries.

Even if you can't fly,

Love still sails ferries.

Let them betray your trust,

But keep your faith intact.

Simply Ideal

31-1-20

Time, on its wings unseen,

Goes flying far and wide.

Killing the beautiful sheen,

Of the smooth, human hide.

My love, darling, so eternal,

As the sun and the moon.

Of course, is like a chapel,

Where you ring a holy tune.

As infinite as an ocean,

Filled with drops of passion.

The heart in my bodily mansion,

Knows nothing but dedication.

Change in nature being vital,

Our bond shall come immortal.

Scvlptor

1-2-20(Sat)

How artistic and intelligent
Is the Creator of Universe!
They made stars magnificent
To adore the heavenly floors.
The energy that from the sun,
Comes giving, life to all.
The earth as a spot of fun,
Where stand trees tall.
To quench the eternal thirst,
Montanes left ice-cold sighs.
Vibrant flora made a tryst,
Symbiosized with seasonal rise.
Animals of infinite Kinds,
Were as the family borne.
All direction sent winds.
Joy in glee, pain scorns.
Glowing Embers:
2-2-20(Sun)
The sword of your memory,

Piercing through my heart;
I resolved to enrich glory,
Our love earned on its part.
The paths spiked with pain,
Tread, I, for the chastity.
Hoping for the soothing rain,
Upon my head as a necessity.
Bodily pleasures we had,
Are but an excellent relic.
Even trouble makes me glad,
When I, our past days cherish.
Come what may, my dearest chick,
Even shall our love tree grow thick.

Betrayal

3-2-20(Mon)
A face with no familiar shape,
Appears before these sunken eyes.
The heart with wounds that gape,
With tears invisible, long cries.
Memories of times of pleasure,
Around the mind, busily hover.
Taking against patience a measue,
That makes even the sky shower.
Those days I wish, I never had,
Filled with love of purest kind.
Sorrow wouldn't have been had,
Where should I old times find?
Not that soul is not alone,
Breath from my body is gone.

Always In Me

Still on my receptive mind,
Imprinted is a pretty face.
Whose resemblance I find,
When at any beauty I gaze.
Never stop ringing in ears,
The sweetest words, she spoke.
My heart full of fears,
How should to her I unlock.
Those sparkling mute eyes,
Asked me many a question.
Lips like the sun at rise,
Moved as rose petals beckon.
Even shall my soul desire,
The one who set it a fire.

Invincible

5-2-20(Wed)
Paths strewn with thorns,
Of pain and associated hurts.
Make efforts of useful scorns,
To stop me from going worlds.
Odds with devilish faces,
Come over to frighten me.
Within me I find braces,
Minted in labs of positivity.
Life at each novel twist,
Brings to me a newchallenge.
Eyes even in blinding must,
Get sharp to see beyond range.
Intoxicated with elixir of hope,
Proceed along the Eternal rope.

Weakened Me

6-2-20(Tue)

I wish I could take away,

Pain in the world today.

And the sorrow in too,

To make humans happily grow.

Then the bitter truth dawns,

And realism strikes, perchance.

God or a savior, not I am,

Wishing impossible is to blame.

Here is what I can do,

Let me know myself through.

A support in times of odds,

To the needy brings wonders.

A resolution, however, do I take,

A kind soul in me to make.

8-2-20(Sat)

Inseparable

In the house of my very soul,
You as ___ lady ______.
When I am on easy stroll,
On each step, you in stride.
Beauty being all over around,
My eyes praise such sights.
Yet never have I found,
Anyone outdoing your light.
No more desires to fulfil,
With you as my holy joy.
Let death my life spill,
Like a kid discarding a toy.
Whatever good and bad I have done,
Living on love made ageing a fun.

Unfortunate

10-2-20(Mon)

You, from me, unbearably far,

Life becomes more than hell.

Nothing but sorrow in store,

Noisy sounds, each chiming bell.

Roses that at me smiled before,

Seem to poke fun at my fate.

Of my sanity, feeling unsure,

Long I for the past recreate.

Living with your memory bitter,

Have I grown to be a living corpse.

Walking like shadows amid litter,

Ever seeking for light of hopes.

Graced shall be the soul of mine,

To avail of a visit, last time.

O Mother Nature, Take me now,

Into your lap, as I am!

Tired of seeing, lying eyes,

Ultimately, Do I seek a flame.

Light of hate being too sharp

To see what has been good.

Solitary Son

11-2-20

In your house of walls,
Do I seek to live forever.
Blessed by your universal love,
Like a child, O Mother Nature,
Under the canopy of moon-light,
On the bed of bare ground.
Sleep shall a blessing be,
Hearing moth's and other sound.
Let your boon of pristine falls,
Be my ideal source of bath.
And fruits, ripened in grace.
The sun will my loneliness warm,
As I am fascinated to your charm.

Pain For The Vain

12-2-20(Wed)

Proud of success and power,

Sat I on the garden fence.

In the mid of windy summer

When dirt flows in dance.

Sailing on the strong gust

From some born, came a stalk.

And entered, my eye fast,

Causing me to cry 'alack'?

Hearing my raising a hell,

Made all family rush to aid.

First hand efforts did fail,

"Call the doctor, mother said.

Even a mere whit of dry grass,

Beat me bad, teaching truth a fresh.

In evitable

13-2-20

My love for your sanity.

Will ever be the same.

Each of my crazy feeling,

Grows to be in passion's flame.

Dreams of us living along,

Are but shadows of truth.

Where in a state of bliss,

Our souls unite in trust.

Eternally shall Love shine,

Like the sun in the sky.

Heating and lighting our lives,

Even though, time does fly.

Beautiful flowers in paradise,

Will go blooming, far and wide.

Coming Home

14-2-20

The bride of peace in me,

Ravaged by miscreahts of vice.

Had me in soul's eye see,

The ruins of a palace nice.

On the wounds given in hate,

Apply, I, balms of affection.

Impatience made me go irate,

When things went odd in fashion.

Inward light being ignored,

Into a dark vale, I sank.

Truth so far in character stored,

Got plundered off life's bank.

O divinity, take me in your hands,

As I am wandering, thro, ghostly lands.

Commemoration

15-2-20

Just over the mango tree,

Where in past we would sit.

A star, I chanced to see.\

Positioned as a mark so fit.

The tree haunted by spirits,

Of lovers, who waited there.

Growing eager with all beats,

Of hearts, that loved fair.

Compassion to the lonely place,

The star to sympathise shone.

Its bright centre, lit by a face,

That could melt even a stone.

Though with pride, I had a smile,

Wiping a tear off my face servill.

Soulful life

17-2-20

The garden of my soul,

Was no less than barren.

Before my heart loved you,

As you resembled an angel.

What joy and sorrow mean,

From ups and downs I knew.

For like a homeless bird,

Tree to tree I would go.

How beautiful life may be,

In your love, this I learnt.

Or soul becomes a hell,

When true hearts be hust.

Trust and most human kind,

Love spreads about in Wind.

Transcendent

22-2-20

Having to keep myself away,
From you, my only life line.
Has been to me but a sky gray,
A contrast to weathers fine.
A frail form of flesh and bone,
Like a humanoid, I now behave.
The soul, now, turned into stone,
Once used to be, a fighter brave.
Waiting earlier for you to come,
To me was a joy with passion,
Wait, still, I to heart the drum,
Death shall beat on my devotion,
Proud of love, will even be my soul,
Never let it neglect the ultimate goal.

Super Cosmic

25-2-20

Despite you being so away,
Love keeps beating in my heart.
Just like the eternal sun,
Brightening the earth on its port.
The heights my soul achieved,
Since you as a star shone.
Are impossible for them to see,
Who let their useless envy drone.
No matter, where bodies are
In this world of beauty fake.
Our souls, in elixir bathed,
Invisible, their pilgrimage make.
Deep within this unbreakable bond.
Lies the beauty, they've never in own.

How, it's OK

26-2-20

A deep inner voice in me,

Tells at times to sing aloud.

No sooner do I tend to,

Than my mind comes around.

Whatever we act or say

In times of sentimental highs.

Keeps chasing us all our life,

Leaving in souls ice cold sighs.

Life shows us colors many,

At various stages in time.

Longing for bright sunshine,

Dies away in scorching clime.

Such thoughts of gloomy kind,

Around my heart, a shackle bind.

Interspersed

27-2-20

All across the pages fine,

Contained in the book of my soul.

A musical song life wine,

Intoxicates me enough to fall.

On a cloud with number nine,

Do I sail through skies.

As clingy as the winding vine,

Never leaving a troll so high.

You in the blood of body

Flow about each vital cell.

Keeping my dauntless ready,

Of our love, to the world tell.

Never shall a day go by,

When you won't be my eyes.

Moon and Shine

28-2-20

Till the day of the world,

Our story shall go around,

Taking its natural twists,

Nowhere boredom will it sound.

Sweet like a candy for kids

Shall appear your face to me.

Deep black eyes, only mine,

Even will smile, in a glory.

A will to live ever together,

Both of us will so nurture.

More promising than paradise,

Will be our love-filled future.

Two lives becoming into one,

Is going to be lover's pun.

Never ending Legend

4-2-20

Even if, there be vast space,

Between our physical beings.

The bell of feelings for you,

In my temple, silently rings.

And you being closest to me,

My life an ecstasy becomes.

Love on its highest peaks,

__fully, my heart so jumps.

Whatever may the case be,

My love, ever grows stronger.

Sad or joyful, matters not,

I wish to go on longer.

The storms of passion in my soul,

Keep me pushing to kick the ball.

A Summer Dream

5-2-20

Playing hide-n-seek with me,

Through the maze of earthly caves.

She on a hill came across,

Searching for me, dazed gaze.

To make a surprising start,

I, pushed her gently forward.

Scream of a railway engine,

Tripped she over me hard.

She hitting me on the face,

I, at her laughed aloud.

That hugging each other tight,

Covered we with cheery shroud.

The soft grass and breeze caressing,

Two bodies got perfectly aligning.

No More Us

6-3-20

Love not around, any more

Life sounds a boring tune.

As dark and as gloomy,

As the sky without the moon.

Flowers though coming a bloom,

To me they seem stall.

Time as usual running on,

My train halts for no rail.

Things pretty not long past,

Appear to be mocking me.

Sorrow eternal taking over,

The home meant for a glee.

Moments spent in joy with you,

Have turned into songs of blues.

6-2-2020

Inseparable

In the house of my very soul

You as thardlady resigned .

When I am on easy stroll ,

On each step you in stride.
Beauty being all over around,
My eyes praise such sights .
10-6-20
On the rails
Of true love .
Run the trains
of life slow
Fuels of freest
Smokeless burning,
The team gives ,
Call whist ling.
The clear path,
Aith tank full ,
The fiery blast ,
An easy pull .
Finish off with journey divine ,
Taking on winds and rains fine.
Monstrous
A vainly furious mind ,

Neves does any good.

With devilish wosd combined,

Turing man to firewood .

Like a knife sharp,

Cutting an apple fast.

Angels dose to a heats,

Pain that long lasts .

Feeding on peaceful soul ,

It soon mighty grows .

Ignosing the Vistue old ,

Winds of Vices blows .

Qualms this fatal fire,

Spraying with divine water.

Betrayed

6-6-20

Crying with sobs,

Like a pet child .

Panics his heat,

In trust beguiled ,

With wings shorn.

Came down Love,

Rose amid thorns.

Stars of ecstary,

Off skies of fate.

Plueked by suspivion,

Of his sout mote .

Curious to groev flowers,

He was in faith robbed .

3-6-20

Eureka :-

The invisible rays ,

Of love divine .

Falling on me,

Paradise is mine.

Other things owned

By fateul karma.

Are but shanes ,

In a staged drama.

Teue joy comes ,

Dropping to souls.

Like at nights,

Dew on roses falls.

No desisres lift for fulfi lment,

To salvation my soul is bent.

Every night in pain ,

And deaths in multitude.

Brought to the union ,

Condemnation and ingratitude.

The lion and the eagle ,

Did convene the kangaroo .

Purposedly making a plan,

To subdue the queer inferno.

Sphere of the living,

Heft behind al most half .

Was by the bold combed ,

In quest of the bluff.

Closed in on all ways ,

Was the cruel dragon beat.

The eagle gorging fiery eyes,

And the lion cheap meat.

Inferior of his isolation,
And devil revenge forced.
The devil from hell's Home
For a suitable chance stored .
Christmas being all around,
The wild were joy billed .
Preps for the feast on,
Rivers too gleeful rilled.
Stole into the kitches ,
The envious yellow monster.
To mix into all dishes,
A fatal indigenous poison .
There was unruly dash,
Amidst the snowy hills.
Of poor innocent guests ,
That were feasting killed.

9 789390 463657